D0097693

THE SUN & MOON SIGNS LIBRARY

TAURUS

APRIL 21 – MAY 21

JULIA AND DEREK PARKER

Photography by Monique le Luhandre
Illustrations by Danuta Mayer

DORLING KINDERSLEY
London • New York • Stuttgart

Dedicated to Gay Hamilton, with love

DK

A DORLING KINDERSLEY BOOK

Editor **Tom Fraser**
Art Editor **Ursula Dawson**
Managing Editor **Krystyna Mayer**
Managing Art Editor **Derek Coombes**
Production **Antony Heller**
U.S. Editor **Laaren Brown**

Computer page make-up Patrizio Semproni.
Photography p 11 by courtesy of the Board of Trustees of the Victoria
and Albert Museum/ Bridgeman Art Library, London; p 16 Tim Ridley.
Stylist pp 28-29 Lucy Elworthy. Illustration pp 60-61 Kuo Kang Chen.
Jacket illustration Peter Lawman. With thanks to
Carolyn Lancaster and John Filbey.

First American Edition, 1992
10 9 8 7 6 5 4 3 2

Published in the United States by
Dorling Kindersley, Inc., 95 Madison Avenue
New York, N.Y. 10016

Library of Congress Catalog Card Number 92-52785
ISBN 1-56458-085-7

Reproduced by GRB Editrice, Verona, Italy
Printed and bound in Hong Kong by Imago

CONTENTS

INTRODUCING
TAURUS

TAURUS, THE SIGN OF THE BULL, IS THE SECOND SIGN OF THE
ZODIAC. IT REPRESENTS A DESIRE FOR STABILITY IN
ALL THINGS, AND AN OVERALL NEED FOR BOTH EMOTIONAL
AND MATERIAL SECURITY.

Taureans like creature comforts, enjoy sweet, rich food, and are very sensual. They make marvelous lovers, but are often too possessive, and can go so far as to treat their partners as if they owned them.

Here, too, is excellent business sense. While not quick to learn, once Taureans absorb a concept, they will seldom forget it.

Traditional groupings

As you read through this book you will come across references to the elements and the qualities, and to positive and negative, or masculine and feminine signs.

The first of these groupings, that of the elements, comprises fire, earth, air, and water signs. The second, that of the qualities, divides the Zodiac into cardinal, fixed, and mutable signs. The final grouping is made up of positive and negative, or masculine and feminine signs. Each Zodiac sign

is associated with a combination of components from these groupings, all of which contribute different characteristics to it.

Taurean characteristics

As the first sign of the earth element, Taurus is characteristically plodding, reliable, and predictable. Being ruled by Venus, however, it also bestows on its subjects great natural charm, and gives them the reputation of being the best-looking Zodiac group.

Taurus is a sign of the fixed quality, so stubbornness can often be present in its subjects. It is therefore very important for Taureans to learn to keep an open mind. Taurus is also, in spite of the symbolic Bull, a feminine or negative sign, which has the effect of inclining its subjects to be introverted.

The Taurean colors are those governed by the planet Venus: pastel blues, pinks, and greens.

ARIES PISCES AQUARIUS CAPRICORN SAGITTARIUS SCORPIO LIBRA VIRGO LEO CANCER GEMINI TAURUS

The Zodiac Wheel

*The relationship between each Zodiac sign
and the traditional astrological groupings
is made clear within the Zodiac wheel. As
you read through this book you will also
discover references to polar, or opposite
signs, and these, too, can be easily worked
out by referring to the wheel.*

FIRE

CARDINAL

EARTH

MASCULINE

MUTABLE

AIR

FEMININE

FIXED

WATER

9

MYTHS & LEGENDS

THE ZODIAC, WHICH IS SAID TO HAVE ORIGINATED IN BABYLON
AS LONG AS 2,500 YEARS AGO, IS A CIRCLE
OF CONSTELLATIONS THROUGH WHICH THE SUN MOVES
DURING THE COURSE OF A YEAR.

The first myth associated with this constellation concerned the Babylonian "Bull of Heaven," Ishtar and Anu, and Gilgamesh, the great epic hero of Babylon.

Ishtar, the goddess of lechery, fell violently in love with the hero Gilgamesh. He knew, however, that she had disposed of her previous lovers in various unpleasant ways, and that she was both faithless and unreliable. Finding herself rejected, Ishtar appealed to her father, Anu, king of the gods, to create a giant Bull of Heaven that would kill Gilgamesh. This bull was Taurus.

A variety of myths

Various other bulls have been associated with the constellation. There was the white bull mentioned by the Roman poet Virgil, which was said to open "the gate of the year with his golden horns." White bulls were also sacrificed at sunset on the fifth day of the Babylonian new year festival, when the equinoctial New Moon appeared in the sign of Taurus.

Europa and the bull

Much better known than this or the Babylonian Bull of Heaven is the bull in the Greek legend of Europa.

Zeus, king of the gods, fell in love with the king of Phoenicia's extraordinarily beautiful daughter, Europa. In order to deceive her into submitting to his dubious intentions, Zeus turned himself into an incredibly handsome bull and set himself to graze among her father's herd. When Europa, who was playing by the seashore with her friends, saw Zeus as the bull, she was overcome by how majestic, yet gentle, he seemed.

The abduction

Europa approached him, and he knelt in front of her. At this, she climbed onto his back, and put a wreath of

Jupiter carries off Europa
In this painting by Pierre Gobert (1662 – 1744), Europa is shown being carried off by the god Zeus, who has disguised himself as a bull.

flowers around his horns. Zeus then sprang immediately to his feet and swam across the sea to Crete. There he had his wicked way with Europa under a plane tree. (This particular tree was then granted the divine privilege of keeping its foliage through all the seasons.) Europa bore Zeus three children. Among them was Minos, who later ruled over the island after the king of Crete, Asterius, adopted all three children and invited Europa to become his wife.

Some traditions of Taurus – the sign of good looks and charm but also of possessiveness – do seem linked to that handsome bull who was really a god in disguise.

TAURUS

SYMBOLISM

CERTAIN HERBS, SPICES, FLOWERS, TREES, GEMS, METALS, AND
ANIMALS HAVE LONG BEEN ASSOCIATED WITH PARTICULAR
ZODIAC SIGNS. SOME ASSOCIATIONS ARE SIMPLY AMUSING,
WHILE OTHERS CAN BE USEFUL.

PRIMROSES

Flowers

*Taurus rules the rose,
primrose, columbine, daisy,
foxglove, poppy, and violet.
The reasons for these
attributions are lost
in the mists of time.*

PINK ROSES

CYPRESS

Spices

Taurus was said by ancient astrologers to rule all spices. Cloves, in particular, fall under the influence of this sign.

Trees

Taurean trees include the ash, cypress, vine, almond, fig, apple, and pear.

Herbs

Spearmint is only one of the herbs traditionally linked to Taurus. Among the others, arrack was used to cure throat infections and elder root for snake bites.

CINNAMON STICKS

SPEARMINT

CLOVES

SYMBOLISM

UNREFINED COPPER

Metal
*The Taurean metal is copper, the
traditional metal of the planet Venus,
which rules the sign.*

COPPER BROOCH

TOY BULL
MADE OF LEAD

Gems

The magnificent emerald and the moss agate are Taurean gems. Their only obvious association with the sign is through their color, green, which is a Taurean color.

MOSS AGATE

EMERALD BROOCH

NINETEENTH-CENTURY BULL CAN-OPENER

SPANISH CERAMIC TILE

Animals

All types of cattle fall under the domination of Taurus.

TAURUS
PROFILE

TAUREANS HAVE THE REPUTATION OF BEING THE BEST-LOOKING
OF ALL 12 ZODIAC TYPES. IF THIS IS TRUE, YOU SHOULD
TRY HARD TO MAINTAIN YOUR APPEARANCE. UNFORTUNATELY,
THIS IS OFTEN A DIFFICULT TASK.

Taureans like to be sure that they are on firm ground, both psychologically and physically. A conventional approach appeals because they prefer established things that are secure and dependable. You are therefore likely to stand with your feet apart, your hands either in your pockets or grasping some all-important possession, for example, a handbag. You will, on the whole, be inclined to present a conventional image of yourself to those around you.

The Taurean face
Your hair is likely to be soft and curly, and may fall well onto your forehead.

The body
Taureans often have a firm, and somewhat stocky, but undeniably handsome, frame. Both men and women tend to be broad-shouldered and to have thick necks, echoing the powerful build of the animal of their sign. They are capable of having slim waists, and must constantly strive to keep themselves in good shape. Flab can, all too easily, mar their natural good looks.

The face
Taureans often have hair that falls well over their foreheads. Soft curls are quite common, and baldness is rarely seen. The forehead itself is likely to be rather low, and as you get older, you may find pronounced horizontal lines appearing there. Your eyes are probably deep-set, dark, and penetrating, but a softness is possibly

The Taurean stance

You will generally adopt a firm stance, with your feet apart, and clasping a favorite possession.

also visible. The Taurean nose is likely to be broad and rather flat, and the chin is is rarely pronounced. Any increase in your weight, and this is something that you should be wary of, may therefore lead to you developing a double chin. Your mouth is likely to reflect your purposefulness, but it can also reveal your sensitivity.

Style

Taureans will dress in a style conventional for their generation. You may therefore have to be careful that your image does not start to look dated. For women, the look tends to prettiness: pastel colors and the occasional frill or bow at the neck. The men will sometimes sport an attractively floral or pastel-colored tie, for example to relieve a formal city suit. The naturally broad shoulders of Taureans usually require a minimum of padding.

In general

The attractive, warm, and sensual speaking voice that is possessed by many Taureans often enhances their

natural good looks. You may have a tendency to move rather slowly and deliberately since, although you are well aware of where you are going, and the way in which you are going to get there, you usually prefer to feel unhurried as you go about your business. Perhaps you should sometimes try speeding up a little, as this might well benefit you both mentally and physically.

TAURUS
PERSONALITY

TAURUS, THE SECOND SIGN OF THE ZODIAC, IS STEADFAST, STABLE,
AND CONVENTIONAL IN OUTLOOK. IT IS IMPORTANT THAT
TAUREANS DO NOT BECOME SLAVES TO A ROUTINE, OR TOO SET IN
THEIR WAYS AND IMMOVABLY STUBBORN.

You are one of the most reliable of all Zodiac types and are also likely to be the most charming. People will soon come to realize that from you they will always be able to expect a warm and affectionate greeting. You have the ability to inspire confidence and will impress everyone with your genuine sincerity.

For you to be completely fulfilled, you must have both emotional and financial security. Indeed, the achievement of this often forms the basic motivation of your life.

At work
You will flourish in a steady, well-paid job, complete with the knowledge that a regular paycheck will be yours. This will enable you to plan your finances with great confidence and let you look toward the future in terms of possessions and purchases. In your case, these will no doubt include a bigger and better house, labor-saving devices to make life easy for you, handsome furniture, and a generally comfortable lifestyle.

Your attitudes
Your need for emotional security is just as strong as your delight in material possessions. There is a danger here, however, since you can unconsciously come to regard your partner as being just another possession. When this happens, the words "my wife" and "my husband" take on quite new – and not altogether pleasant – connotations. More is said on this subject elsewhere (*see pages 26 – 27*), but the tendency must be underscored. Possessiveness is by far the worst Taurean fault, and this is the most dangerous area in which it can be expressed.

Material things, for example your home and its furniture – in fact most objects a Taurean can own – may also become too important to you, just like

Venus rules Taurus

Venus, the Roman goddess of love, represents the ruling planet of Taurus and Libra. The influence of Venus extends to art and fashion, and relates to the feminine side of a Taurean's nature.

the figures in your bank balance. The trait relates, of course, to your need for security.

The overall picture

Taureans are very often passionate people with strong feelings and opinions. Luckily, you usually express your powerful emotional level in a positive way. Like the Taurean bull, however, while you may be slow to anger, once roused your rage is often considerable. Be magnanimous, and learn to reject resentfulness.

With your liking for the good life, there is a chance that you may feel a conflict between the necessity to work hard, in order to attain that prosperous, luxurious lifestyle, and a certain indulgent laziness.

TAURUS
ASPIRATIONS

FOLLOWING A REGULAR ROUTINE WILL NOT WORRY YOU. YOUR
ORGANIZATIONAL AND MONEY-MAKING SKILLS MAY
HELP YOU TO START YOUR OWN BUSINESS. DO NOT BE AFRAID
OF TAKING OCCASIONAL RISKS.

COIN BALANCE

Finance
*A career in finance may suit
money-loving Taureans.
They will usually take great
care when investing.*

COINS

Arts and crafts
*As an earth sign, Taurus has a strong feeling
for natural materials. Taureans enjoy using
wood or clay, and a variety of fabrics.*

DIVIDERS AND
ARCHITECTURAL PLAN

POLISH BEADWORK

Architecture
*Taureans have a strong sense of
balance and form. They often
design buildings that have an
affinity with the landscape.*

The wine trade
Most Taureans love wine and are discriminating connoisseurs. Some will enjoy making it, either from grapes or from other natural ingredients that come to mind. Restaurant management may appeal.

ITALIAN
BOTTLE
OPENER

The theater
Theater work may not provide the security that many Taureans need, but they can be great musicians.

The beauty industry
Taureans like working in the luxury trades, perhaps as beauticians. Their love of nature demands that they use goods produced without harming animals.

BEAUTICIAN'S
TOOLS

GREASEPAINTS

TAURUS

HEALTH

BECAUSE OF THEIR LIKING FOR RICH FOOD, OFTEN COMBINED WITH
A SLOW METABOLISM, MANY TAUREANS HAVE A TENDENCY
TO PUT ON WEIGHT EASILY. THEIR NECKS AND THROATS ARE
VULNERABLE TO INJURY OR INFECTION.

Although Taureans are generally disciplined people, they sometimes find the routine of exercise difficult to maintain.

Your diet

As a Taurean, you no doubt love your food. If you have a slow metabolism, you should therefore do what you can to speed it up, perhaps through exercise, to help you fight weight gain. You may need to supplement your diet with sodium sulfate (nat. sulph.), which helps to eliminate excess water from the body.

Taking care

It should be kept in mind that the planet Venus rules not only the sign Taurus, but also the thyroid gland. If, therefore, you are considerably overweight for no apparent reason, you should think about being tested for possible thyroid inactivity.

The Taurean body area is the throat and neck, so you should take care to sleep with a suitable pillow. You may otherwise find yourself waking up with a stiff neck.

Grapes

Among the foods traditionally associated with Taurus are grapes, cereals, berries, and beans.

Astrology and the body

For many centuries it was not possible to practice medicine without a knowledge of astrology. In European universities, medical training included information on how planetary positions would affect the administration of medicines, the bleeding of patients, and the right time to pick herbs and make potions.

Each Zodiac sign rules a particular part of the body, and early medical textbooks always included a drawing that illustrated the point.

TAURUS AT LEISURE

Each of the Sun signs traditionally suggests spare-time activities. Although these hobbies and vacation spots are only suggestions, they often suit Taurean interests and tastes.

Gardening
Taurus is an earth sign and has always been associated with gardening, especially the creation of beautiful flower gardens.

GARDENING EQUIPMENT

Comfortable hotel stays
Taureans need and enjoy their creature comforts. When you are on vacation, you no doubt like to relax in the luxury of an expensive hotel.

BRASS HOTEL KEYS

Embroidery
*Taureans are often patient, with a
fondness for detail. Meticulous work such
as model-making, craftwork, or
embroidery will no doubt fascinate you.*

PASTRY CUTTER

ROLLING PIN

Cookery
*Although this hobby is normally
associated with Cancerians, many
Taureans enjoy baking cakes and
making desserts.*

POSTAGE
STAMPS

Travel
*You hate uncertainty and, having found
your ideal vacation destination, you are
likely to return there regularly. It could be
Ireland, Cyprus, the Greek islands,
Iran, or Switzerland.*

Sport
*Team sports might be fun
when you are young, but
these are likely to be
replaced by games of skill,
like bowling.*

BOWLING BALLS

LOVE

WHEN A TAUREAN IS IN LOVE, THE INFLUENCE OF VENUS
RULES THE DAY. UNDER THESE CIRCUMSTANCES, YOU
WILL EXPRESS YOUR VERY BEST CHARACTERISTICS IN A WAY
THAT CANNOT FAIL TO IMPRESS A LOVED ONE.

You may, with your overwhelming need for emotional security, find it hard to step into the vast unknown of a new relationship. Taureans need to be very sure of their partners before making any commitment to them. The worst Taurean fault is possessiveness and, when you are in love, this tendency can be quite vehemently expressed. You may find yourself thinking: "You're mine – all mine!" Together with a tendency to cling, this may create a claustrophobic atmosphere that will put many other Sun signs off. Allowing a partner a little more freedom will be much more productive.

Taureans are very generous lovers, and your gifts may have a good investment value. Naturally, this means that you are investing in your lover's emotions, in anticipation of a long-lasting relationship; but you are also looking to the future in a more material way. If, by some misfortune, the pair of you should fall upon hard times, the gift could be sold.

As a lover

Sexually, you are likely to be an admirable lover. Every move that you make will be unhurried, and every act of love will be

beautifully paced, with consideration for your partner's needs. Joy and passion will combine to the satisfaction of you both. Without a doubt, all Taureans are capable of being exciting lovers. The best kind of Taurean lover is, of course, one who can be both protective and caring.

Types of Taurean lover
Some Taureans can be surprisingly oversensitive. Many of you are nostalgic and may tend to look to the past in a rather sentimental way. This could be a little difficult for a lively, forward-looking partner to cope with. Others of your Sun sign are prone to be more assertive; their passion is intense and fiery. They must take care not to expose a selfish streak that could mar a relationship. There are also those people who express their love in a pure Taurean way, by recognizing every one of the traits that are set out here and by learning to counter any negative possessiveness. Some of you tend to have a flirtatious side to your nature, which lightens Taurean passion. This group tends to be talkative and requires partners with active minds as well as lively bodies.

TAURUS AT HOME

COMFORT IS THE KEYNOTE OF A TAUREAN HOME, WITH TRADITION
BEING THE BACKBONE OF THE FURNISHING AND DECOR. WARM
PINK OR PALE BLUE COLORS MAY PREDOMINATE. ABOVE ALL, THE
ATMOSPHERE WILL BE CALM AND CUSHIONED.

Taureans usually have an overall need to feel secure. A typical Taurean home will be beautiful, large and, above all, very comfortable. This may even be motivated by a conscious effort to show how comfortably placed its inhabitants are. The perfect Taurean house will have a yard, and will preferably be located in the country. If this is not possible, then a quiet suburb should suffice just as easily. When you take time to sit down and relax in your living room, you will want to feel the warmth and the security of a solid, but luxurious and very comfortable armchair.

Your choice of furniture is likely to tend toward the conventional and, if this is the case, you will probably

Elegant flower display
*The Taurean home is very
likely to boast at least one
beautiful display of flowers.*

prefer to choose styles that will not date too easily. Wildly fashionable articles are unlikely to hold much appeal for you; you will, in general, want your furniture to be easy on the eye, and very welcoming. It is likely that your furniture will be extremely pretty, perhaps containing soft, delicate shades of pink, blue, and perhaps some very pale green, which are the colors of Venus, the Taurean ruling planet.

Decorative objects
Since most Taureans love flowers, there is a fair chance that you will own plenty of beautiful vases in which to put them. Taureans sometimes have a

Music stand and flute
*If, like many Taureans, you play an
instrument, you may give it pride of place.*

perhaps in a glazed cotton or shiny
satin. Frills often abound in the
Taurean home, and there will be a
proliferation of sheers to enhance
windows, or to block out any
uninteresting view outside. These
will, however, be kept pulled right
back if you have a beautiful flower
garden of which you are justifiably
proud. You probably prefer thick
carpets, and will use beautiful rugs
not only to preserve your carpets, but
decoratively, in their own right, to
enhance the look of your home.

collection of books on gardens or
gardening. Alternatively, you might
accumulate business magazines (some
Taureans enjoy thinking about
finance as much as gardening).

Soft furnishings
Taureans often obtain terrific
pleasure from choosing new drapes
and cushions. You will, more than
likely, decide upon floral patterns,

Comfortable armchair
*The floral pattern on this comfortable
armchair is typically Taurean.*

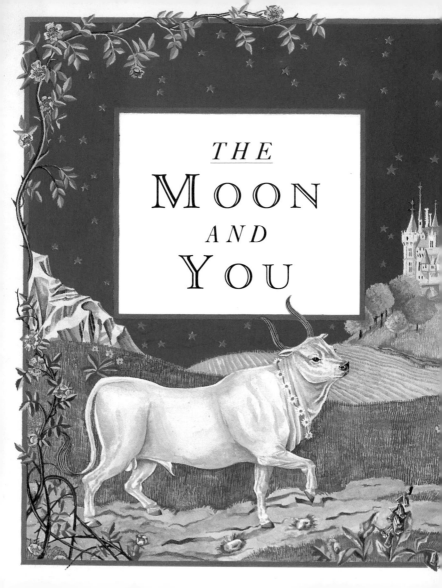

THE
MOON
AND
YOU

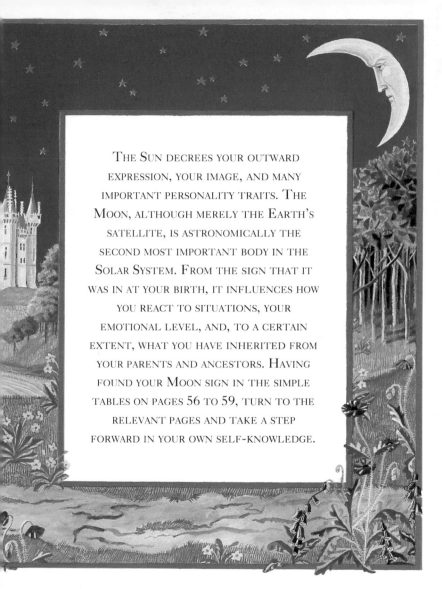

THE SUN DECREES YOUR OUTWARD
EXPRESSION, YOUR IMAGE, AND MANY
IMPORTANT PERSONALITY TRAITS. THE
MOON, ALTHOUGH MERELY THE EARTH'S
SATELLITE, IS ASTRONOMICALLY THE
SECOND MOST IMPORTANT BODY IN THE
SOLAR SYSTEM. FROM THE SIGN THAT IT
WAS IN AT YOUR BIRTH, IT INFLUENCES HOW
YOU REACT TO SITUATIONS, YOUR
EMOTIONAL LEVEL, AND, TO A CERTAIN
EXTENT, WHAT YOU HAVE INHERITED FROM
YOUR PARENTS AND ANCESTORS. HAVING
FOUND YOUR MOON SIGN IN THE SIMPLE
TABLES ON PAGES 56 TO 59, TURN TO THE
RELEVANT PAGES AND TAKE A STEP
FORWARD IN YOUR OWN SELF-KNOWLEDGE.

THE MOON IN
ARIES

ARIES IS A FIRE SIGN, SO YOUR REACTIONS TO SITUATIONS ARE
ENTHUSIASTIC AND OFTEN EMOTIONAL: UNDER PRESSURE
YOU COULD TAKE HASTY OR PREMATURE ACTION. MAKE AN EFFORT
NOT TO SUPPRESS YOUR TAUREAN CAUTION.

Your Arien Moon enables you to respond to situations with enthusiasm and speeds up your reactions. You could occasionally act hastily, and your Moon could even allow you to take some risks.

Self-expression
Taureans are generally warm people, and because your Arien Moon also provides a highly charged emotional influence, you will have a particularly high emotional level. You will be quick to anger, and may find it a little difficult to get along with some people. But because of the speed with which the Moon works when in Aries, you can throw off anger, and dismiss any outpouring of emotion, more easily than many Taureans.

Romance
You will be a very passionate lover, and because of an element of Moon sign impatience – something that is

virtually unknown to Taureans – you may tend to sweep partners off their feet. You are also less likely to succumb to Taurean possessiveness.

If you have a greater need for independence and freedom than most Taureans, do not ignore this. You most certainly have a very lively zest for love and sex which, coupled with warm Taurean sentiment and affection, plus your delightful sensuous qualities, makes you a wonderful lover.

Your well-being
The effect of an Arien Moon on your health could be to render you prone to headaches. If you suffer from them frequently, do not ignore the possibility that you may be suffering from a minor kidney problem.

You should also remember that Aries is an accident-prone sign and that, through carelessness, you may sometimes cut or burn yourself. If

The Moon in Aries

your responses to situations tend to be hurried, or you are prone to flurries of hastiness, there is a distinct possibility that you could be very vulnerable in this respect.

Planning ahead

Your Taurean business sense may be impeded by your Arien Moon. While it will encourage you to invest your money, you may do so a fraction less wisely than your Taurean Sun sign would have it. You may have a

sneaking regard for quick, risky growth, and could end up learning the hard way – by losing money.

Parenthood

You will be a less conventional, and perhaps less strict, parent than with many Taureans. You will understand when your children wish to express their independence. You will also manage to sidestep the Taurean tendency to spoil them. Encourage family members to exercise plenty.

THE MOON IN
TAURUS

WITH BOTH THE SUN AND THE MOON IN TAURUS AT THE TIME
OF YOUR BIRTH, YOU WERE BORN AT THE TIME OF THE
NEW MOON. AS AN EARTH SIGN, TAURUS POWERFULLY
INFLUENCES YOUR PERSONALITY AND REACTIONS.

Should you study a list of your Sun sign characteristics, you will probably recognize that a great many of them apply to you. On average, out of a list of perhaps 20 traits of a Sun sign listed in books or magazines, most people will strongly identify with 11 or 12. In your case, however, the average increases considerably because the Sun and Moon were both in Taurus when you were born.

Self-expression
Your Sun sign makes you cautious, methodical, and not given to rushing around; your Moon sign encourages you to respond to situations in the same careful manner.

Your Taurean need for security is extremely strong, and your need for emotional security is perhaps second to none. You need a steady routine, like most people of your Sun sign, but with you it goes deeper than that. If, for instance, your schedule is unexpectedly disrupted, you will not find it easy to adjust, and your whole system could suffer.

You may fly into a rage more frequently than other Taureans, and this does not always have positive results: Try to emerge from this type of mood as quickly as you can.

Romance
You can be a wonderfully responsive Taurean lover, as long as you consciously check what may amount to a fatal flaw of being possessive. You could, without thinking, make life claustrophobic for your lover; if accused of this, you should take the rebuke seriously.

Your well-being
Healthwise, you must watch a tendency to put on weight; losing it may not be easy for you. One solution is to try to increase your metabolic rate, which may be naturally slow. For

The Moon in Taurus

instance, try walking a little more quickly and climbing stairs instead of relying on elevators.

Planning ahead

You may be something of a wizard at making money and at stretching your income much further than might seem possible. You have an excellent instinct for investment: Your cautiousness and tendency to go for steady growth ensure that you get the best possible results from your portfolio. Financial risk-taking is not

something to which you are normally prone. You do, however, love luxury and creature comforts and will therefore be wise to earn as much money as you possibly can.

Parenthood

While making sure that your children have the best of everything, you may veer between being too strict and spoiling them. They may have more independent spirits than you; do not try to quell this. A show of affection will endear you to them.

THE MOON IN
GEMINI

YOUR GEMINIAN MOON PROVIDES YOU WITH UNUSUALLY RAPID RESPONSES TO SITUATIONS. SHOULD YOU SUFFER FROM RESTLESSNESS, ALLOW YOUR TAUREAN STABILITY TO CALM IT. ANY SUDDEN IDEAS COULD BE VERY ORIGINAL.

Your lighthearted Geminian Moon makes you both original and capable of conveying your ideas to other people easily. You are, no doubt, an excellent communicator, and in all kinds of situations will respond to others in an open, friendly way. You are probably more talkative than many Sun sign Taureans.

Neighboring Zodiac signs are always very different, and from Gemini the Moon gives your stable, down-to-earth Taurean character some delightfully contrasting Geminian facets.

Self-expression

Gemini is not a highly emotional sign, and your reaction to most situations may be remarkably cool and detached. It could also be well spiced with a questioning logic.

But it is likely that, having first been affected by your Geminian Moon, your Taurean qualities soon

take over. When your Sun sign dominates, you do anything to get what you want, just the way you want it. In your case stubbornness, supported by verbosity, will definitely come into its own from time to time.

Romance

Your Moon sign will make you express your natural charm and affection in a delightfully flirtatious way. You will enchant and attract lovers, who will not have to wait long to know how you feel about them.

You need a certain freedom of expression in this sphere of your life. Although your Taurean possessiveness may make it difficult, you must also recognize that your partners may need some freedom, too.

Your well-being

The Geminian body area covers the arms, hands, and lungs. In your case, a sore throat could well be followed by

The Moon in Gemini

a chest cough. If the cough persists, do not ignore it, since it could develop into something more serious. Your metabolism is probably considerably faster than that of most Taureans, so a susceptibility to putting on weight could be less of a problem for you. You should enjoy exercise.

Planning ahead

You may not be quite as cautious or as interested in steady financial growth as many Taureans. From time to time you could fall for some enticing get-rich-quick scheme, with awful results. Do not always follow your first reactions to such schemes.

Parenthood

You will have fewer problems with the generation gap than is usual with Taureans, because any Geminian influence encourages one to be future-oriented. In your case it will add a certain youthfulness of outlook that will help you to respond well to the concerns, opinions, and needs of the younger generation.

THE MOON IN
CANCER

WITH THE MOON IN CANCER, YOUR AFFECTIONATE QUALITIES
ARE COMBINED WITH TENDER, CARING EMOTION. YOU
WILL EXPRESS THIS POSITIVELY TO YOUR LOVERS AND FAMILY. BE
SENSIBLE IF YOU ARE SEIZED BY AN IRRATIONAL WORRY.

Earth and water are complementary elements, and the power of your Cancerian Moon (it is strong because the Moon rules Cancer) will vie for expression with your Taurean Sun. Therefore your Taurean qualities will be very powerfully affected by protective instincts. Your need for emotional security, which is so much a part of your Taurean motivation, will also be strongly enhanced and extended toward your loved ones.

Self-expression

All Taureans are practical and have plenty of common sense. Those with the Moon in Cancer have great intuitive foresight and will instinctively know when the time is right to be determined and brave.

You will achieve much, but may be a little undisciplined in your approach to life, sometimes allowing yourself to do what your prevailing mood seems to dictate. Beware of mood swings that could hamper your progress. You have a wonderful imagination, but practical though you are, it is easy for you to succumb to worry. If your imagination takes over, you can really work yourself into a frenzy.

Your emotional resources are considerable, and you should be able to find plenty of outlets for them in all areas of your life.

Romance

You will be a romantic, perhaps even sentimental lover, capable of expressing your feelings tenderly, and you will be sensitive and responsive to your partner's needs. It may, however, be difficult for you to come to terms with the circumstances of the breakup of a relationship.

Your well-being

The chest and breasts are the Cancerian body areas, but so, to a certain extent, is the digestive system.

The Moon in Cancer

Worry is likely to cause problems in the latter area and, as a Taurean, your liking for good food and wine can exacerbate them. You can put on weight all too easily and may well have to constantly discipline yourself to a very strictly controlled diet. The best forms of exercise for you are swimming and, as has already been suggested, dance.

Planning ahead

Taurean possessiveness and the Cancerian need to hoard things work in two ways. In the first instance you can be shrewd, intuitive, and practical. But in the second, you may hoard things, and your portfolio could become cluttered with unprofitable investments. Develop an enterprising spirit that will allow you to progress.

Parenthood

As a caring parent who wants the very best for your children, do not be over-protective or possessive. This could be very difficult for you, and at times you may tend to talk about life as it was when you were a child. Try seeing the world through your children's eyes, because it will help you to avoid the generation gap.

TAUREANS AND THOSE WITH THE MOON IN LEO LOVE COMFORT
AND LUXURY. AS A RESULT, YOU MAY SPEND PLENTY OF MONEY
IN ORDER TO ENJOY THEM. DEVELOPING YOUR NATURAL GOOD
BUSINESS SENSE WILL HELP SUPPORT SUCH INDULGENCES.

Your powers of observation are enhanced by your Leo Moon, which gives you the ability to take command of almost any situation with only the briefest notice.

Self-expression

Your Taurean Sun makes you extremely reliable and full of common sense. People will take it for granted that you can cope well with any situation. In fact, they may easily tend to take advantage of these qualities – not that you will really mind. Knowing what your priorities are, you will rise above any pettiness and spend your time rewardingly.

Both Taurus and Leo are of the fixed quality, and as a result, not only can you be pretty stubborn at times, but you may also find it difficult to change your opinions.

Leo is a fiery, enthusiastic, and passionate sign, so your response to situations will be spiced with great emotion. Express your enthusiasm freely, especially in relation to your personal interests and hobbies.

Romance

When you are in love, your emotions should flow both positively and quite delightfully. You will be as lavish in expressing your feelings toward your partners as you will be in ensuring that you enjoy every possible luxury that you can, or perhaps really cannot, afford. Leos are naturally generous, and your Leo Moon makes you particularly responsive to such pleasures as beautiful, expensive evenings spent entertaining yourself and your lover.

Your well-being

The Leo body areas are the spine and back. If you have a sedentary job, get a well-designed chair to keep it in good order. The Leo organ is the heart. To benefit it, perhaps you

The Moon in Leo

should try walking or jogging regularly. Or you could work out at a pleasant, comfortable health club.

Your Taurean tendency to gain weight could be increased by the influence of Leo. If your Moon sign attracts you to exercise, it can only be a good thing.

Planning ahead

Where money is concerned, your needs are substantial. While you may be satisfied with a regular paycheck, you are unlikely to be very fulfilled by a lifestyle that does not allow you to enjoy your work and take pride in

it. Think about this carefully: Money is, indeed, important, but so is your inner contentment.

Parenthood

You will work hard for your children and do a lot for them, but you must ensure that you allow them to develop in the way that they want to. Do not be overpossessive, or try to make them into clones of yourself. Provided they have one or two compelling interests, that is all they need. If you also make an effort not to be bossy, you will minimize any problems associated with the generation gap.

THE MOON IN
VIRGO

WITH THE SUN AND MOON BOTH IN EARTH SIGNS, YOU ARE A VERY
PRACTICAL PERSON. DO NOT LET APPREHENSIVENESS OR
A LACK OF SELF-CONFIDENCE SPOIL YOUR TAUREAN ENJOYMENT
OF LIFE AND ITS SENSUAL PLEASURES.

The combination of your Sun and Moon signs makes you among the most practical of Taureans. Your Moon sign is, however, not noted for self-confidence, and this may have tended to inhibit you, especially when you were a child.

Self-expression

A certain shyness may have made you very quiet when you were young. Conversely, however, you may have become nervously talkative when you felt self-conscious. Attaining a balance and allowing the inner stability of your Taurean Sun to shine through may be something you have consciously had to develop.

Both Taurus and Virgo are of the earth element – hence your strong practical qualities. At the physical level, contact with the earth may mean a lot to you. Perhaps you love gardening, or can grow beautiful indoor plants. The countryside is probably important to you, so if your career holds you to a city center, try to live near a park, or escape out of town as often as possible.

Romance

You are a good communicator and must never hold back and fail to express your real feelings. This is especially true when you are in love. Do not cramp the wonderful Taurean way in which you express yourself, or your warm, tender passion.

You may also have an uncharacteristic tendency to be overly critical of your loved ones. Bear in mind that while well-founded constructive criticism may be helpful, carping and nagging are not.

Your well-being

The Virgoan body area is the stomach and, to some extent, the nervous system. When you are worried, it may be your stomach that reacts first.

42

The Moon in Virgo

You definitely need a high-fiber diet, to counter the effects of Taurean indulgence in rich food. If you suffer from a buildup of tension, you could find yourself prone to migraines.

Planning ahead

Virgoans are careful with money, and for you, that carefulness works at an instinctive level. This is helpful, since Taureans can be too generous. Virgoans often find it embarrassing to be generous. You will certainly find

nothing ostentatious in owning property; Taurus will balance you in this respect.

Parenthood

You may well have a natural ability to teach your children, so that by the time they go to school they will be well on the way to reading. Be proud of their efforts. As in all of your dealings, remember that you have the capacity to be far more critical than you might realize.

THE MOON IN
LIBRA

As they are both ruled by Venus, Libra and Taurus have a great deal in common. Your Libran Moon will encourage you to respond very well to everything that Taureans find attractive.

Although Taurus is an earth sign and of the fixed quality, and Libra an air sign and of the cardinal quality, they still have much in common. Above all, they share charm.

Self-expression
You find it very easy to convey the warmth of your Taurean personality with your instinctive and strong measure of tact and diplomacy. However, just because your Libran influence makes it easy to persuade people to your way of thinking, you must not stifle your Taurean common sense. Otherwise, you may end up using people. Anyone with a strong Libran influence also tends to be indecisive. When the occasion demands it, let Taurus take control.

Romance
With the Moon in Libra, you will possess a romantic air. You will express your feelings freely and

gracefully, without overwhelming your lover by too sudden an approach. Your courtship will lead gently but firmly from romance to passion.

Notorious Taurean anger is less likely to erupt openly in you than in many Sun sign Taureans. Your instincts incline you to peace at any price, and you will always try to resolve problems diplomatically.

Your well-being
The Libran body area is the kidneys, and any upsetting circumstances can cause a kidney imbalance that might lead to headaches.

The Taurean love of a relaxed lifestyle is echoed by your Moon sign – so you may need to be very strict with yourself if you start a new exercise program or a diet. It may pay for you to exercise at a good health club, where saunas and steam rooms offer both a relaxing and a sociable time. It would be best for you to avoid

44

The Moon in Libra

crash diets completely. Instead, very gradually teach yourself to stop eating any highly calorific foods.

Planning ahead
Compared to most Taureans, you may not have the same urge for making money. You will, however, enjoy spending it. Any spare money must therefore be invested wisely, so that as you get older, you will be able to afford more luxuries. If you are looking for extra money, selling beauty products might be a good idea.

Obtain sound professional financial advice before investing your savings, but do tell your advisor about any ideas you may have. You will learn a lot in the process and grow confident about managing your own affairs.

Parenthood
You could get a little tired of your children's demands for attention, so try to arrange to have a few hours away from them each week. Always make sure that your children know where they stand with you.

THE MOON IN
SCORPIO

TAURUS AND SCORPIO ARE POLAR OR OPPOSITE SIGNS, WHICH
MEANS THAT YOU WERE BORN UNDER A FULL MOON.
BEWARE OF RESTLESSNESS, AN UNCHARACTERISTIC TRAIT
AMONG TAUREANS, AND TRY NOT TO ACT JEALOUSLY.

Each of us is, in one way or another, apt to express the attitudes of our polar, or opposite, Zodiac sign. Each sign has its partner across the horoscope; for you this is Scorpio. Furthermore, as the Moon was in Scorpio when you were born, this "polarity" (as it is known) will emerge in a very interesting way.

Self-expression
Scorpio is very highly charged with emotional and physical energy. You will therefore react strongly when you meet with a challenge. Those born under Taurus are placid enough until rage gets the better of them, but your powerful polar qualities will join forces in your personality not only when you are angry, but also when you are moved in any way.

It is very important that you try to fill your days with tasks and events that make demands on your physical energy and also provide you with psychological fulfillment. Most people born at the time of the Full Moon tend to suffer occasionally from an element of restlessness or inner discontent. In your case, you must always be on guard against this.

Romance
The chief Taurean fault, possessiveness, is related to a Scorpio weakness – jealousy. In terms of your emotional relationships, this means that while they are likely to be highly charged (and you will no doubt contribute to that), jealousy can occur. It is always a good idea to discuss problems with your partners, but do not do this if your intuition leads you to explode into anger before you are sure of your facts.

Your well-being
The Scorpio body area covers the genitals, and these, along with your Taurean throat, are vulnerable. "Safe

The Moon in Scorpio

sex" and regular testicular exams for men or gynecological visits for women are important for you.

You may easily put on weight, especially if your metabolism is on the slow side. If this is the case, try to engage in some exercise.

Planning ahead
The Taurean business sense and liking for possessions and material security marries well with similar Scorpio qualities. In your case,

however, because of the Moon's influence, you also have a considerable instinct for bargains and investments. You should follow it.

Parenthood
You will work hard for your family, but you could be more strict, and more insistent on somewhat harsh discipline, than you realize. Try to be aware of this, especially when your children want to move out and start living their lives in their own ways.

THE MOON IN
SAGITTARIUS

FACED WITH A CHALLENGE, YOU WILL FIND YOURSELF RESPONDING
ENTHUSIASTICALLY. USE THIS ENTHUSIASM TO YOUR
ADVANTAGE, AND DO NOT SUPPRESS IT WHEN YOUR TAUREAN
CAUTION STRIVES TO TAKE OVER.

Your fiery Sagittarian Moon adds many contrasting facets to your steady, more cautious, earthy Sun sign. You respond much more quickly to situations than do many people of your Taurean Sun sign.

Self-expression
Your mind is always open to challenge, once excited by an idea or a project, you will immediately want to get involved. This can be a good thing, but it can also work slightly to your disadvantage: overoptimism is a Sagittarian problem that has to be contained. Luckily, in your case, after your initial enthusiasm, your Taurean caution usually takes over.

Romance
Your intense Taurean emotions are enlivened by your Moon sign, and while, like all Taureans, you need both emotional and material security, within a relationship you also need an element of independence. This sits uneasily with your Taurean tendency to be possessive. You may well resent your partners intensely for being possessive of you, but at the same time, act just as possessively toward them. If you are accused of this, take heed. Your Sagittarian enthusiasm and passion for life will color your attitude to love just as much as they do other areas.

Your well-being
The Sagittarian body area covers the hips and thighs. Sagittarius is yet another sign that enjoys rich food, in particular hefty casseroles, but the predilection for sweet desserts is less marked than in Taureans. Taurean women with a Sagittarian influence will have a tendency to gain weight on their hips and thighs.

The Sagittarian organ is the liver, and indigestion can be a problem. Upsets in this area are common

The Moon in Sagittarius

enough after a Taurean night out, but if you also have a Sagittarian Moon? No more need be said.

Sagittarians often enjoy sports with an element of daring. Fortunately, however, your Taurean caution will let you enjoy such activities safely.

Planning ahead

A similar sneaking regard for risk-taking can emerge in your attitude toward money, where your instincts can encourage you to invest too heavily. The thought of large spoils will attract you but, in the end, you might encounter disaster. Try not to

learn the hard way. Think things out before you act. In this area, always rely on your Taurean nature.

Parenthood

You will be less conservative than many Taurean parents. Your lively response to your children's questions and demands will be gladly received, and you are capable of getting really enthused by their interests. Make sure that you take time out to have fun with your children, as well as spending your hard-earned money on them. For you, the generation gap should not prove to be a problem.

THE MOON IN
CAPRICORN

YOU HAVE AN AMBITIOUS STREAK AND SHOULD PURSUE YOUR
ASPIRATIONS AS FAR AS YOU CAN. USE YOUR TAUREAN
COMMON SENSE AND CAUTION, BUT DO NOT LET THEM CRAMP THIS
VITAL URGE — IT IS YOUR PATH TO INNER FULFILLMENT.

The earth element is important to your psychological makeup: Both Taurus and Capricorn are earth signs. So when you read about Taurean practical common sense and caution, you will immediately recognize these traits in yourself.

Self-expression
Are you ambitious and aspiring, or do you fail to progress in life as much as you would like to? The latter is fine if you are managing to achieve inner fulfillment; but surely you cannot be happy with simply trundling along in the same old rut, year after year. Of course, you could experience a mixture of times when you are successful, and others when you lack self-confidence and tend to hold back.

If you feel that other people are cramping your style – or for that matter, that you are doing so yourself – remember that caution and common sense are the best building blocks,

and that your Moon sign, while causing fluctuations in your responses to challenges, can also allow you to take steady strides toward bigger and better things.

Romance
Capricorn is a cool, unemotional sign, so some of your Taurean ardor will probably be stifled. Capricorn is, however, also a faithful sign, and therefore complements your Taurean qualities excellently.

One tendency of which you should be aware is a susceptibility to social climbing. This may not work well for your emotional life, whatever it does for your social position. Your heart should decide in these matters.

Your well-being
The Capricornian body area covers the knees and shins, and the bones. If you are sluggish and experience periods when you positively shun

The Moon in Capricorn

sports or other exercise, your joints could suffer. You should also make sure that you have regular dental checkups, especially if you have a Taurean sweet tooth, since Capricorn also rules the teeth.

Planning ahead

Taureans are generous, and love luxury and comfort. Capricornians are entirely the opposite. In fact, their tastes can be positively Spartan; this might cause some internal conflict that will need resolving. You should

be pretty good with cash, making wise investments that show a regular, steady growth.

Parenthood

Bringing work home from the office in order to make extra money for your children's education might not be a good idea. Your concern for their material well-being may mean that they lack both affection and pleasure. Also try not to be too much of a disciplinarian; you are fair, but you may be stricter than you realize.

THE MOON IN
AQUARIUS

YOUR AQUARIAN WISH TO BE UNCONVENTIONAL AND TO STAND
OUT FROM A CROWD COULD CLASH WITH A TAUREAN NEED
TO CONFORM. TRY TO UNDERSTAND THIS STRUGGLE; DEVELOP
CREATIVE ORIGINALITY AND CHECK STUBBORNNESS.

Although they are essentially very different, Taurus and Aquarius share the same fixed quality. Stubbornness, for example, is a characteristic common to all Taureans, and in your case it is exacerbated by your Aquarian Moon.

Self-expression
It is particularly important that you recognize your potential to be stubborn. Try to remember that firmness is one thing, but a closed mind is another.

Your Aquarian Moon also lends some unusual and lively qualities to your Taurean Sun. You are, for instance, among the least conventional of a sign that tends to adhere strictly to convention. You will often surprise your friends by reacting in ways that they do not expect. This is not a bad thing, since it gives you a certain attractive sparkle. Remember that your unconventional streak can,

however, make you unpredictable, and that your reactions may be inconvenient to other people.

Romance
Aquarius is not a highly emotional sign, and your Taurean passion will to some extent reflect this. However, an Aquarian enthusiasm for romance will reveal itself, to great effect, in your expression of love and sex.

You have an independent spirit and may need more freedom of expression than many Sun sign Taureans. Do not, therefore, rush into a permanent relationship or marriage. In fact, you could well have a lot to come to terms with in your love life.

Your well-being
The Aquarian body area is the ankles, so take extra care if you go skiing or skating, or decide to wear high-heeled shoes. Aquarius also rules the circulation and, while you will tend to

The Moon in Aquarius

enjoy cold, crisp weather, make sure that you keep warm; your circulation may not be too good. You could enjoy karate as a form of exercise.

Planning ahead
Financially, you may be less shrewd than many Taureans. You could be attracted to showy but not very sound investments, so be cautious, and do not gamble more than you can afford to lose. Furthermore, you are often drawn to buy interesting and unusual items for your home or wardrobe, which may be expensive and too fashionable to be wise investments.

Parenthood
It is important that your children know where they stand with you. If they do not, because you change your mind too often, you could end up causing a lot of family tension. Encouraging your children to be interested in unusual and intriguing hobbies comes easily to you.

THE MOON IN
PISCES

YOU ARE SYMPATHETIC, WITH A NEED TO OFFER OTHERS A HELPING
HAND. LET TAUREAN COMMON SENSE TAKE OVER, HOWEVER,
BEFORE YOU GIVE TOO MUCH MONEY AWAY. YOU ARE A WONDERFUL
LOVER, BUT BEWARE OF BEING TOO POSSESSIVE.

Your earth sign Taurean Sun and water sign Piscean Moon blend well. As a result, your reactions to situations are both sensitive and emotional; you respond in a very caring, sympathetic way.

Self-expression

While you are practical, your inner strength and toughness are less apparent. This is particularly true when you meet with a challenge, in that you are sometimes not as assertive or as determined as other Sun sign Taureans.

Beware of a tendency to take the easy way out of difficult situations, which could be caused by a lack of confidence. Should this be the case, think of all your past achievements and give yourself more credit.

Pisceans tend to put on rose-colored glasses at the least provocation, while Taureans usually face up to reality. A little dreaminess

will not come amiss, especially when heightened by the imaginative creativity that could be an integral part of your potential.

Romance

Taurean affection and sensuality blend well with Piscean emotion, making you a wonderful lover. You should, however, beware of falling for someone too quickly, since when you meet with reality, you may come down to earth all too rapidly.

It should not be too difficult to keep Taurean possessiveness at bay, but your Piscean Moon could cause you to be deceitful in tricky situations, perhaps because you are choosing the easiest way out.

Your well-being

The Piscean body area is the feet. You may find it difficult to get shoes that fit well, or you might simply be glad to take them off and go barefoot

The Moon in Pisces

whenever possible. Like Taurus, Pisces is a sign prone to weight gain – perhaps because Pisceans get thoroughly bored when checking the calorie content of foods. Allow your gourmet tendencies their freedom, but do not fall back on junk food any more than is absolutely necessary.

Planning ahead
Kindness and sympathy, and a desire to help, may place a strain on your bank balance. Try to keep a practical outlook when someone tells you a heartrending story. Always discuss investments with an expert so that your rather impractical Piscean response to financial matters will not damage or smother your sound Taurean business sense.

Parenthood
You will make a wonderful, caring parent, who will be sensitive to your children's needs. Use your imagination not only to inspire and encourage the development of their potential, but also to help you express and develop your own. Any creative work that you do with them, for instance photography or dance classes, will be good for all of you.

MOON CHARTS

REFER TO THE FOLLOWING TABLES TO DISCOVER YOUR MOON SIGN.
THE PRECEDING PAGES WILL TELL YOU ABOUT ITS QUALITIES.

By referring to the charts on pages 57, 58 and 59 locate the Zodiacal glyph for the month of the year in which you were born. Using the Moon table on this page, find the number opposite the day you were born that month. Then, starting from the glyph you found first, count off that number using the list of Zodiacal glyphs (below, right). You may have to count to Pisces and continue with Aries. For example, if you were born on May 21, 1991, first you need to find the Moon sign on the chart on page 59. Look down the chart to May; the glyph is

Sagittarius (♐). Then consult the Moon table for the 21st. It tells you to add nine glyphs. Starting from Sagittarius, count down nine, and you find your Moon sign is Virgo (♍).

Note that because the Moon moves so quickly, it is beyond the scope of this little book to provide a detailed chart of its positions. For more detailed horoscopes, you will need to consult an astrologer, but if you feel that this chart gives a result that does not seem to apply to you, read the pages for the signs either before or after the one indicated; one of the three will apply.

MOON TABLE

DAYS OF THE MONTH AND NUMBER OF SIGNS THAT SHOULD BE ADDED

DAY	ADD	DAY	ADD	DAY	ADD	DAY	ADD
1	0	9	4	17	7	25	11
2	1	10	4	18	8	26	11
3	1	11	5	19	8	27	12
4	1	12	5	20	9	28	12
5	2	13	5	21	9	29	1
6	2	14	6	22	10	30	1
7	3	15	6	23	10	31	2
8	3	16	7	24	10		

ZODIACAL GLYPHS

♈	Aries
♉	Taurus
♊	Gemini
♋	Cancer
♌	Leo
♍	Virgo
♎	Libra
♏	Scorpio
♐	Sagittarius
♑	Capricorn
♒	Aquarius
♓	Pisces

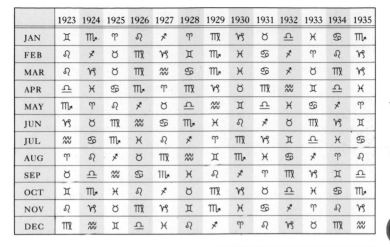

	1923	1924	1925	1926	1927	1928	1929	1930	1931	1932	1933	1934	1935
JAN	♊	♏	♈	♌	♐	♈	♍	♑	♉	♎	♓	♋	♏
FEB	♌	♐	♉	♍	♑	♊	♏	♓	♋	♐	♈	♌	♑
MAR	♌	♑	♉	♍	♒	♋	♏	♓	♋	♐	♉	♍	♑
APR	♎	♓	♋	♏	♈	♍	♑	♉	♍	♒	♊	♎	♓
MAY	♏	♈	♌	♐	♉	♎	♒	♊	♎	♓	♋	♐	♈
JUN	♑	♉	♍	♒	♋	♏	♓	♌	♐	♉	♍	♑	♊
JUL	♒	♋	♏	♓	♌	♐	♈	♍	♑	♊	♎	♓	♋
AUG	♈	♌	♐	♉	♍	♒	♊	♏	♓	♋	♐	♈	♌
SEP	♉	♎	♒	♋	♏	♓	♌	♐	♈	♍	♑	♊	♎
OCT	♊	♏	♓	♌	♐	♉	♍	♑	♉	♎	♓	♋	♏
NOV	♌	♑	♉	♍	♑	♊	♏	♓	♋	♐	♈	♌	♑
DEC	♍	♒	♊	♎	♓	♌	♐	♈	♌	♑	♉	♍	♒

	1936	1937	1938	1939	1940	1941	1942	1943	1944	1945	1946	1947	1948
JAN	♈	♌	♑	♉	♍	♒	♊	♎	♓	♌	♐	♈	♍
FEB	♉	♎	♒	♊	♏	♈	♌	♐	♉	♍	♑	♊	♎
MAR	♊	♎	♒	♋	♐	♈	♌	♐	♉	♎	♒	♊	♏
APR	♌	♐	♈	♌	♑	♉	♎	♒	♋	♏	♓	♌	♑
MAY	♍	♑	♉	♎	♒	♊	♏	♓	♌	♐	♉	♍	♒
JUN	♎	♒	♋	♏	♈	♌	♑	♉	♎	♒	♊	♏	♓
JUL	♏	♈	♌	♑	♉	♍	♒	♊	♏	♓	♌	♐	♈
AUG	♑	♉	♎	♒	♋	♏	♈	♌	♐	♉	♍	♑	♊
SEP	♓	♋	♏	♈	♌	♑	♉	♍	♒	♋	♏	♓	♌
OCT	♈	♌	♑	♉	♎	♒	♊	♎	♓	♌	♐	♈	♍
NOV	♊	♎	♒	♊	♏	♈	♌	♐	♉	♍	♑	♊	♏
DEC	♋	♏	♓	♌	♑	♉	♍	♑	♊	♎	♒	♋	♐

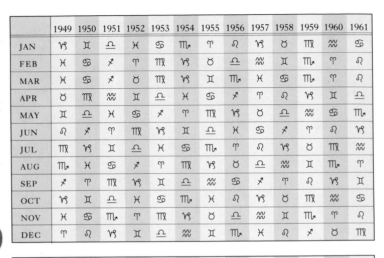

	1949	1950	1951	1952	1953	1954	1955	1956	1957	1958	1959	1960	1961
JAN	♑	♊	♎	♓	♋	♏	♈	♌	♑	♉	♍	♒	♋
FEB	♓	♋	♐	♈	♍	♑	♉	♎	♒	♊	♏	♈	♌
MAR	♓	♋	♐	♉	♍	♑	♊	♏	♓	♋	♏	♈	♌
APR	♉	♍	♒	♊	♎	♓	♋	♐	♈	♌	♑	♊	♎
MAY	♊	♎	♓	♋	♐	♈	♍	♑	♉	♎	♒	♋	♏
JUN	♌	♐	♈	♍	♑	♊	♎	♓	♋	♐	♈	♌	♑
JUL	♍	♑	♊	♎	♓	♋	♏	♈	♌	♑	♉	♍	♒
AUG	♏	♓	♋	♐	♈	♍	♑	♉	♎	♒	♊	♏	♈
SEP	♐	♈	♍	♑	♊	♎	♒	♋	♐	♈	♌	♑	♊
OCT	♑	♊	♎	♓	♋	♏	♈	♌	♑	♉	♍	♒	♋
NOV	♓	♋	♏	♈	♍	♑	♉	♎	♒	♊	♏	♈	♌
DEC	♈	♌	♑	♊	♎	♒	♊	♏	♓	♌	♐	♉	♍

	1962	1963	1964	1965	1966	1967	1968	1969	1970	1971	1972	1973	1974
JAN	♏	♓	♌	♐	♈	♍	♑	♊	♎	♒	♋	♐	♈
FEB	♐	♉	♍	♒	♊	♏	♓	♋	♏	♈	♍	♑	♉
MAR	♐	♉	♎	♒	♊	♏	♈	♌	♐	♉	♍	♑	♊
APR	♒	♋	♏	♈	♌	♑	♉	♍	♒	♊	♏	♓	♋
MAY	♓	♌	♐	♉	♍	♒	♊	♎	♓	♋	♐	♈	♍
JUN	♉	♎	♒	♊	♏	♓	♌	♐	♉	♍	♑	♊	♎
JUL	♊	♏	♓	♌	♐	♈	♍	♑	♊	♎	♓	♋	♐
AUG	♌	♐	♉	♎	♒	♊	♏	♓	♋	♏	♈	♍	♑
SEP	♍	♒	♋	♏	♓	♋	♐	♉	♍	♑	♊	♎	♓
OCT	♏	♓	♌	♐	♈	♍	♒	♊	♎	♒	♋	♐	♈
NOV	♐	♉	♎	♒	♊	♎	♓	♋	♐	♈	♍	♑	♉
DEC	♑	♊	♏	♓	♋	♐	♈	♌	♑	♉	♎	♒	♊

	1975	1976	1977	1978	1979	1980	1981	1982	1983	1984	1985	1986	1987
JAN	♌	♑	♉	♍	♒	♊	♏	♓	♌	♐	♉	♍	♑
FEB	♎	♒	♋	♏	♈	♌	♐	♉	♍	♒	♊	♎	♓
MAR	♎	♓	♋	♏	♈	♍	♑	♉	♎	♒	♊	♏	♓
APR	♐	♈	♍	♑	♊	♎	♒	♋	♏	♈	♌	♑	♉
MAY	♑	♉	♎	♒	♋	♏	♓	♌	♐	♉	♍	♒	♊
JUN	♓	♋	♐	♈	♌	♑	♉	♎	♒	♊	♏	♓	♌
JUL	♈	♌	♑	♉	♍	♒	♋	♏	♓	♌	♐	♉	♍
AUG	♉	♎	♓	♋	♏	♈	♌	♐	♈	♎	♒	♊	♎
SEP	♋	♐	♈	♌	♐	♊	♎	♒	♊	♏	♓	♌	♐
OCT	♌	♑	♉	♍	♒	♋	♏	♓	♋	♐	♉	♍	♑
NOV	♎	♓	♋	♏	♓	♌	♐	♉	♍	♒	♊	♎	♓
DEC	♏	♈	♌	♐	♉	♍	♑	♊	♎	♓	♋	♐	♈

	1988	1989	1990	1991	1992	1993	1994	1995	1996	1997	1998	1999	2000
JAN	♊	♎	♒	♋	♏	♈	♌	♑	♉	♎	♒	♊	♏
FEB	♋	♐	♈	♍	♑	♉	♎	♒	♋	♏	♈	♌	♐
MAR	♌	♐	♉	♍	♒	♊	♎	♓	♋	♏	♈	♌	♑
APR	♍	♒	♊	♏	♓	♋	♐	♈	♍	♑	♊	♎	♓
MAY	♏	♓	♌	♐	♈	♍	♑	♉	♎	♒	♋	♏	♈
JUN	♐	♉	♍	♑	♊	♎	♓	♋	♐	♈	♌	♑	♉
JUL	♑	♊	♎	♒	♋	♐	♈	♌	♑	♉	♎	♒	♋
AUG	♓	♌	♐	♈	♍	♑	♉	♎	♓	♋	♏	♓	♌
SEP	♉	♍	♑	♊	♏	♓	♋	♏	♈	♌	♑	♉	♎
OCT	♊	♎	♒	♋	♐	♈	♌	♑	♉	♎	♒	♊	♏
NOV	♌	♐	♈	♍	♑	♉	♎	♒	♋	♏	♈	♌	♑
DEC	♍	♑	♉	♎	♒	♋	♏	♈	♌	♐	♉	♍	♒

THE
SOLAR SYSTEM

THE STARS, OTHER THAN THE SUN, PLAY NO PART IN THE SCIENCE
OF ASTROLOGY. ASTROLOGERS USE ONLY THE BODIES IN THE
SOLAR SYSTEM, EXCLUDING THE EARTH, TO CALCULATE HOW OUR
LIVES AND PERSONALITIES CHANGE.

Pluto
Pluto takes 246 years to travel around the Sun. It affects our unconscious instincts and urges, gives us strength in difficulty, and perhaps emphasizes any inherent cruel streak.

Neptune
Neptune stays in each sign for 14 years. At best it makes us sensitive and imaginative; at worst it encourages deceit and carelessness, making us worry.

Uranus
The influence of Uranus can make us friendly, kind, eccentric, inventive, and unpredictable.

Saturn
In ancient times, Saturn was the most distant known planet. Its influence can limit our ambition and make us either overly cautious (but practical), or reliable and self-disciplined.

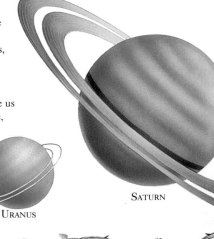

SATURN

PLUTO

NEPTUNE

URANUS

Jupiter

Jupiter encourages expansion, optimism, generosity, and breadth of vision. It can, however, also make us wasteful, extravagant, and conceited.

Mars

Much associated with energy, anger, violence, selfishness, and a strong sex drive, Mars also encourages decisiveness and leadership.

JUPITER

MARS

Earth

Every planet contributes to the environment of the Solar System, and a person born on Venus would no doubt be influenced by our own planet in some way.

The Moon

Although it is a satellite of the Earth, the Moon is known in astrology as a planet. It lies about 240,000 miles from the Earth and, astrologically, is second in importance to the Sun.

MERCURY

THE MOON

VENUS

EARTH

The Sun

The Sun, the only star used by astrologers, influences the way we present ourselves to the world – our image or personality the "us" we show to other people.

Venus

The planet of love and partnership, Venus can emphasize all our best personal qualities. It may also encourage us to be lazy, impractical, and too dependent on other people.

Mercury

The planet closest to the Sun affects our intellect. It can make us inquisitive, versatile, argumentative, perceptive, and clever, but maybe also inconsistent, cynical, and sarcastic.